BELLEW, PETER

CALDER

4/82

CALDER

H.L.

Published by Chartwell Books Inc.
A Division of Book Sales Inc.
110 Enterprise Avenue
Secaucus, New Jersey 07094

ISBN 0-89009-448-9
Library of Congress Catalog Card Number: 81-66870

Printed in Spain by La Polígrafa, S. A.
Dep. Legal: B. 12.097-1981

Peter Bellew

CALDER

CHARTWELL BOOKS INC.

FOTOSCOP
VISUAL LANGUAGE

Photographs: Clovis Prevost

Selection and sequence: J. Prats Vallès

"Là je vois de près et de loin
Là je m'élance dans l'espace
Le jour la nuit sont mes tremplins
Là je reviens au monde entier
Pour rebondir vers chaque chose
Vers chaque instant et vers toujours
Et je retrouve mes semblables."

(Paul Eluard, "Poésie ininterrompue")

Poet and musician are indivisible and poetry is music. The eye of the poet is innocent and true and it is in the eye of the poet that dreams are born.

The eye of Calder reflects the blue of a cloudless sky which is his canvas – his domain. The day and the night are the springboards from which he projects his visual music upwards to remain in space, moving or motionless –*mobile* or *stabile*– in defiance of gravity. Dream satellites of metal, forged with the precision of the engineer and shaped with the sensibility and intensity of the poet.

Poet of movement, poet of the sky, his mobiles twist, turn, revolve –or remain immobile awaiting the wind's embrace– in a marriage of motion and unity. Each element, time, motion, space, as interdependent as time, sound and silence are in music.

To ask what is a Calder is to ask what is a composition of Mozart, what is a tree, a flower, a mountain. For those who cannot hear there is only void – for those who cannot see, only darkness.

To be in Calder's studio is like attending the rehearsal of a symphony orchestra – the air is charged with fragments of music. The deafening notes of the brass, the slender notes of the woodwinds here, the magic of the strings there. One is immediately confused, even deafened, by the disorder, but one's senses are aroused, excited and sharpened in a manner impossible elsewhere. A direct contact with the composer's material is made – a participation which enables one not only to appreciate his final work but also, and more importantly, to enter into his inner spirit.

Like the man himself, Calder's art is of today – the XXth century. It is revolutionary, not evolutionary, uniquely bound to its epoch, firstly by the nature of its raw materials and secondly by the spirit of its creator.

Calder has little interest in the past, its history or its vestiges. To tradition he pays scant, if any, attention either in his life or his work. The well-proved, the established, the secure bore, not to say irritate, him. Age does not impress him nor the words of the wise. He loves the experimental and uncertainty – his impatience is for the morrow and the yet-to-be-born. He is an adventurer into the unknown and, as befitting his time, his eyes were turned from the beginning of his career to the conquest of space. Before the astronauts had circled the world, he, in his own manner, had already made it his own. His earliest wire sculptures and circus drawings show this preoccupation – space encircled to express solids – and with the birth of his first mobiles, he created a new celestial universe.

"J'ai le sublime instinct de la pluie et du feu
J'ensemence la terre et rends à la lumière
Le lait de ses années fertiles en miracles
Et je dévore et je nourris l'éclat du ciel."

(Paul Eluard, "Poésie ininterrompue")

In his life, as in his work, modesty, tensile strength and liberty are dominant. Everything is open and meant to be seen – to be experienced. In his studio, and his house, doors are rarely closed, never locked. Winter and Summer, windows remain open to the sky inviting wind and man to enter. Objects he has collected have been chosen not for their monetary value or rarity but for their form, their colour, their purpose. Almost all are made of the most primitive, simplest and lightest materials – Japanese paper kites, multi-coloured tin-foil Arab lanterns, Brazilian feathered toys, flimsy tin, French weathercocks from farm-house roofs – all reflectors of light and all designed to be seen in space. Hanging from beamed ceilings, standing without arrangement on tables, chairs and window sills, his mobiles turn, stop and recommence.

But it is when they are in repose that the quintessence of Calder is most truly sensed – in those instants when movement is threatened rather than present his full magic is revealed.

> *Je parle et l'on me parle et je connais l'espace*
> *Et le temps qui sépare et qui joint toutes choses*
> *Et je confonds les yeux et je confonds les roses*
> *Je vois d'un seul tenant ce qui dure ou s'efface.*

> (Paul Eluard, "Poésie ininterrompue")

BIOGRAPHY

1898   Born in Philadelphia (Pennsylvania), U.S.A. His grandfather and his father were sculptors, his mother, Nanette Lederer, a painter.

His family lived, successively, in Arizona, California and New York State.

1915   Calder studies engineering in the Stevens Institute of Technology, in Hoboken, New Jersey. He achieves the highest marks ever given in descriptive geometry.

1918   Is called up and serves in the navy.

1919   Graduates as a Mechanical Engineer. First engineering job.

1920-1923   Calder works on a St. Louis newspaper, signs on as a sailor on a freighter, becomes timekeeper in a logging camp. At the same time, he draws: in New York, he attends drawing classes at night school. At the logging camp he sends for a paint-box, in order to paint the «stumps of the trees and the mountains».

1923-1926   Back in New York, Calder attends drawing and painting classes in the Art Students League, while working as an engineer in public works and the building trade.

For the National Police Gazette —which is actually a satirical review— he does sports sketches and a report on the Barnum circus.

1926   He publishes «Animal Sketching», holds his first exhibition of paintings and does his first sculpture: «The Flattest Cat».

In the month of June he signs on again on a freighter, in July he visits Paris, in August he returns to New York and in September he returns again to Paris, where he begins the «Circus» and does his first sculptures in wire, which are representations of Josephine Baker.

1927-1928 The first performances of the «Circus», an ensemble of articulated personages, objects and animals, take place in Paris and have a certain success, thanks to the presence of personalities like Jean Cocteau.

During 1927, Calder exhibits animated toys at the «Salon des Humoristes». He paints some pictures and does his first sculptures in wood.

He spends his time between Paris, where he makes the acquaintance of Miró, and the United States, where he exhibits wire sculptures.

1929 Exhibitions in Paris and the United States. Calder does his first sculptures in bronze, his first pieces of jewellery and his first «animated constructions», which are the earliest form of his mobiles.

1930 Calder sails for Spain on a freighter, then visits Corsica and the South of France on a small yacht.

The performances of the «Circus» become more and more successful. Among the spectators are: Varèse, Painlevé, Léger, Einstein, Le Corbusier, Mondrian... Calder says to Duchamp: «I should like to make Mondrians that move...» He does some abstract paintings.

1931 Marries Louisa James, by whom he is to have two daughters. Meets Jean Arp and Hélion, joins the «Abstraction-Création» movement, illustrates Aesop's Fables and exhibits «abstract» sculptures.

1932 First exhibition, at the Galerie Vignon, of 30 constructions with animation and sound, half of which are fitted with motors. Marcel Duchamp christens them «Mobiles». By way of contrast, Jean Arp is to give the name of «Stabiles» to the sculptures not intended to move.

1933 Constructs his first motorless mobiles, which are moved by the movements of the air. Exhibits in a group show with Arp, Hélion, Pevsner, Miró, Seligmann. Buys a farm, which he still possesses, at Roxbury in Connecticut.

1934 First exhibition at the Pierre Matisse Gallery, New York.

1935-1936   Calder does décors for two ballets by Martha Graham and for «Socrate» by Eric Satie.

1937   For the Spanish pavilion at the Paris International Exhibition, Calder constructs his celebrated «Fountain of Mercury».

1938-1942   Calder works, exhibits and travels. One exhibition, in New York in 1940, is devoted exclusively to jewellery.

1943   He does his «constellations», compositions in wood and wire.

The New York Museum of Modern Art organizes an important retrospective exhibition of his works and J. J. Sweeney writes a study of him.

The first work to carry the name of Stabile in his catalogue is done this year. It is the «Morning cobweb» in painted sheet-iron.

1944   J. P. Sartre writes a celebrated preface for an exhibition of mobiles at the Galerie Louis Carré in Paris.

1945-1949   Numerous exhibitions (the Kunsthalle of Berne, the Stedelijk Museum of Amsterdam, Rio de Janeiro, São Paulo). Calder does mobiles for dance spectacles.

1950   First exhibition at the Galerie Maeght. Calder carries out Stabile-Mobiles, which he distinguishes from the «Standing mobiles», and in 1951 he does some «Towers».

1952   Grand prize for sculpture at the Venice Biennale. Décors for Pichette's «Nuclea», presented at the T.N.P.

1953   Buys a house at Saché, near Tours. From 1960 on he is to stay for ever longer periods there, though in 1957 he also buys a house in Brittany, near Tréguier.

1958-1960   Calder does some lithographs. In the following years, apart from his jewellery sculpture, he is to work on engravings, tapestries, paintings and numerous *gouaches*.

1961 . Constructs «4 elements» (10 metres high), moved by motors, for the Moderna Museet of Stockholm. Film on the «Circus» by Carlos Vilardebo.

1962 Calder has a large studio built on a hill near his house at Saché.
He executes a giant stabile (18 metres) for the town of Spoleto.
Michel Butor writes a poem for an exhibition of *gouaches* in Paris.
Cartoons for tapestries.

1964 The stabile «Renforts» for the Maeght Foundation at St.-Paul-de-Vence.
Retrospective exhibition at the Guggenheim Museum New York.

1965 Retrospective exhibition at the National Museum of Modern Art, Paris.

1967 Calder constructs more and more «Giant stabiles». For the Montreal World Fair he creates «Man», 22 metres in height.

1968 Calder works on another creation, of the same kind, for the Mexican Olympic Games.
Exhibition at the Galerie Maeght.

1969 April 2nd, retrospective exhibition at the Maeght Foundation in St.-Paul-de-Vence.

ILLUSTRATIONS

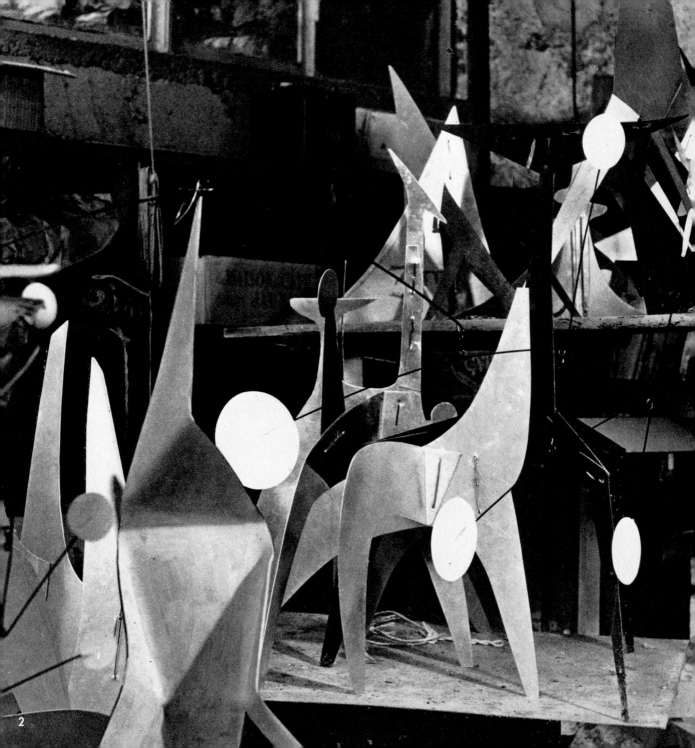

4

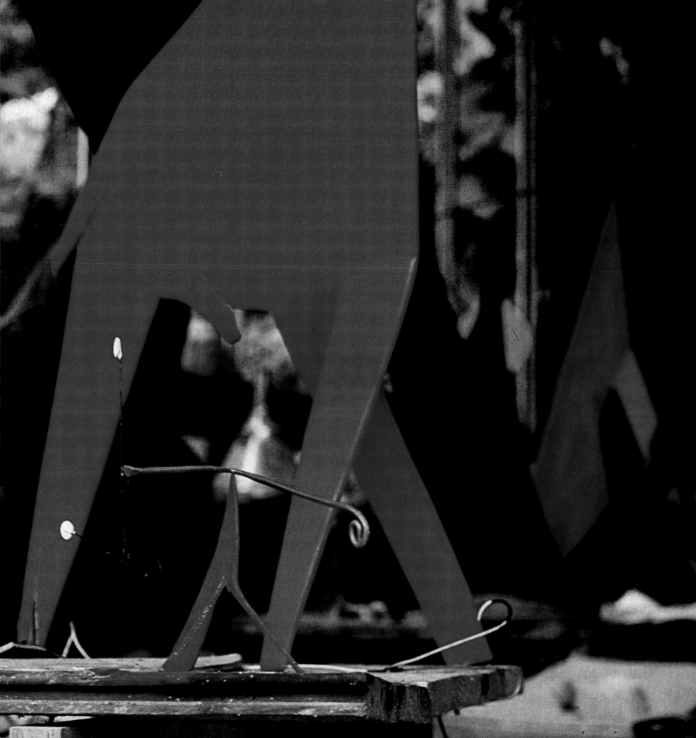

8

1

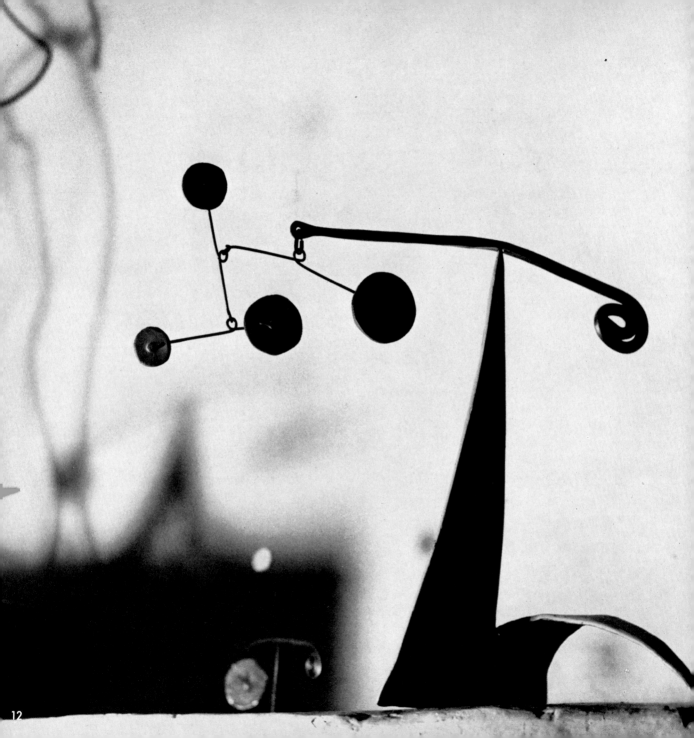

13

15

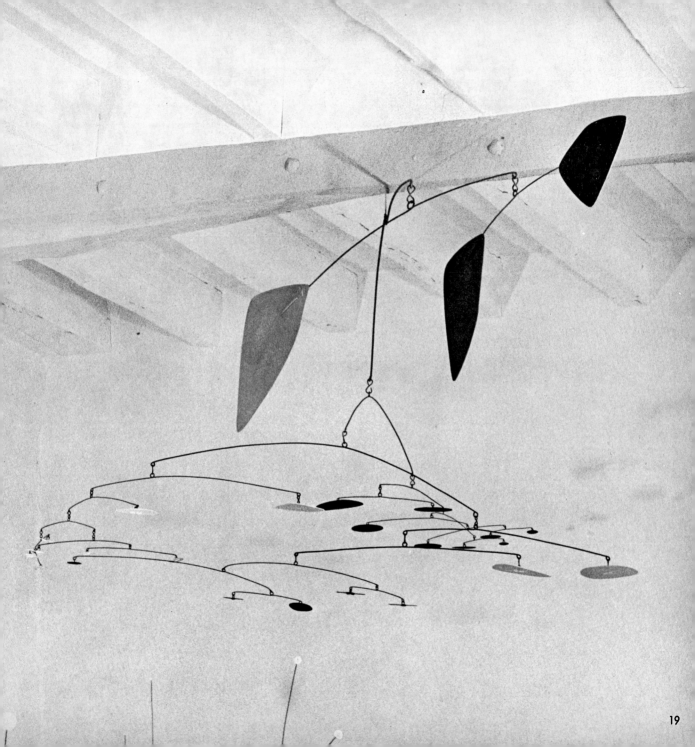

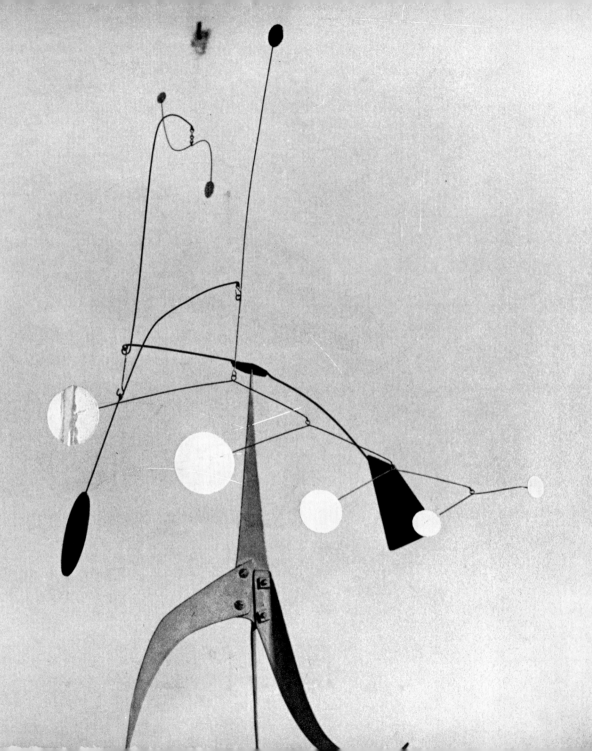

29

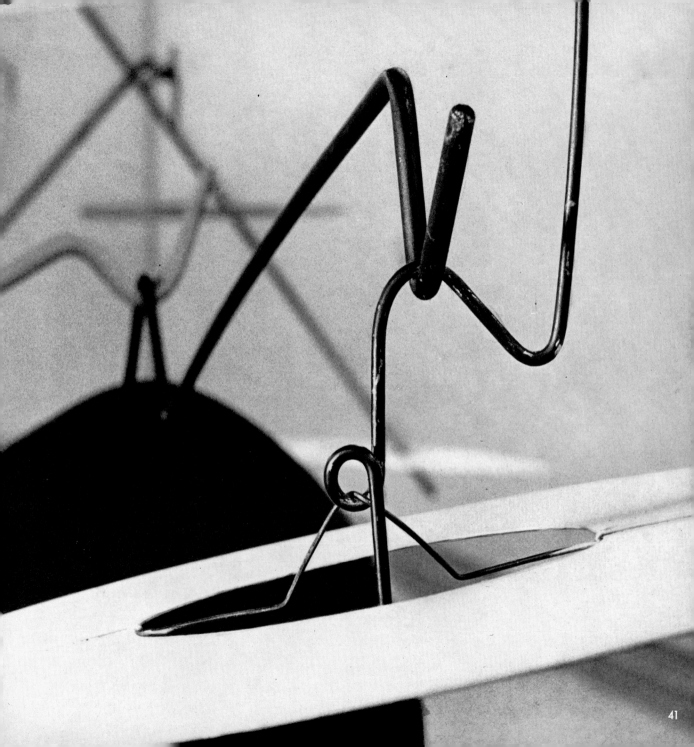

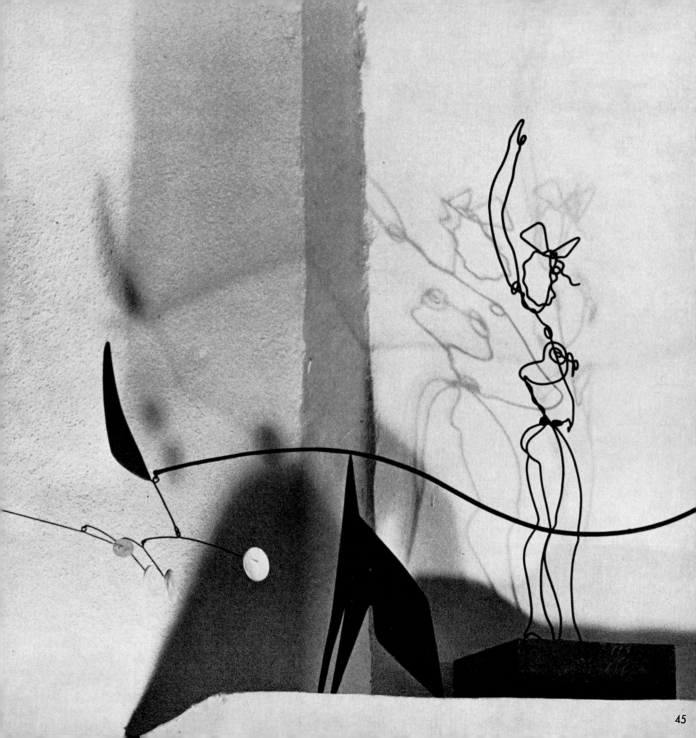

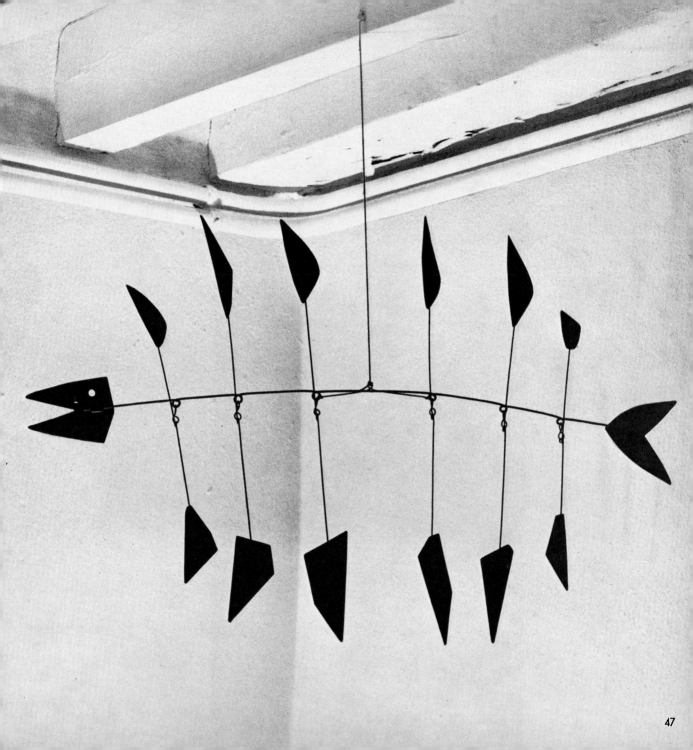

49

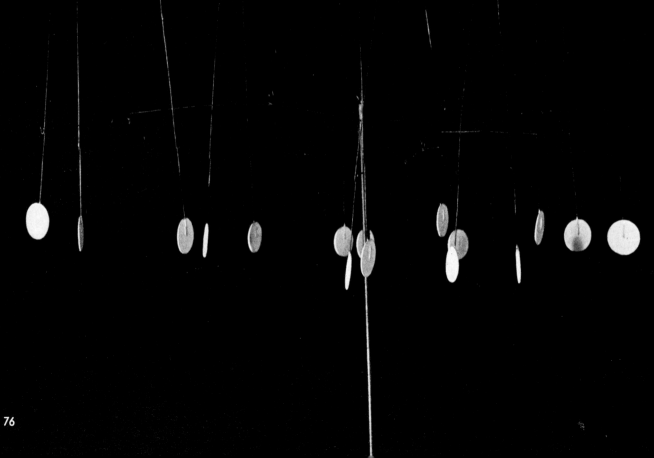

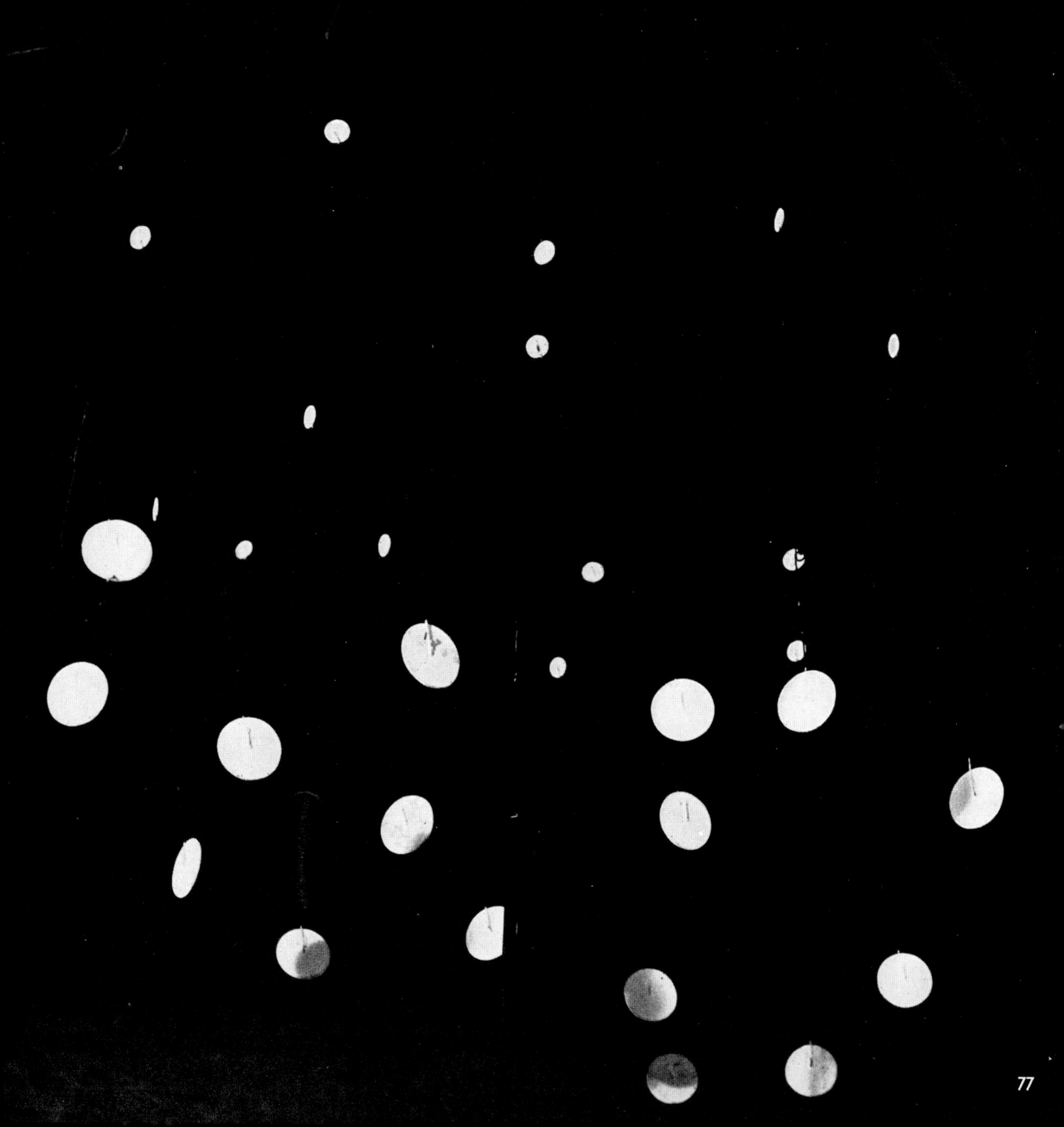

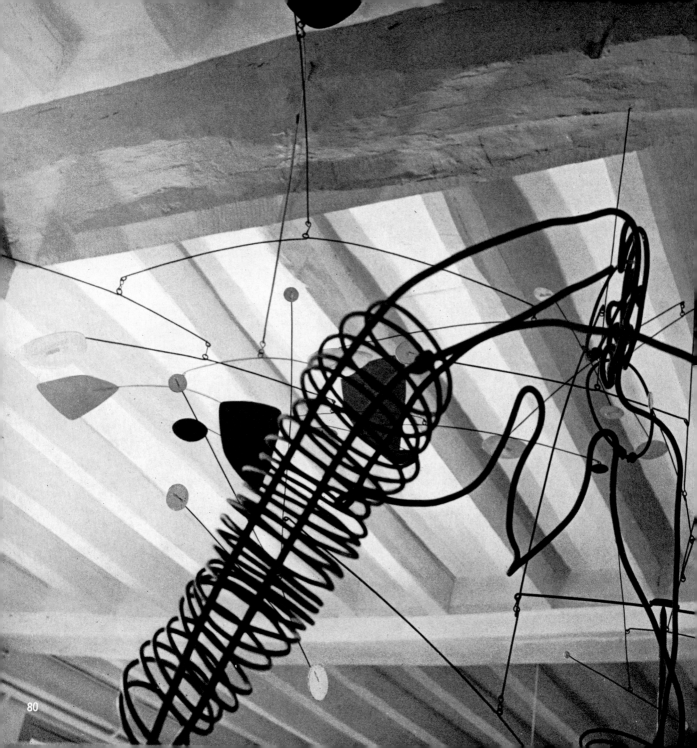

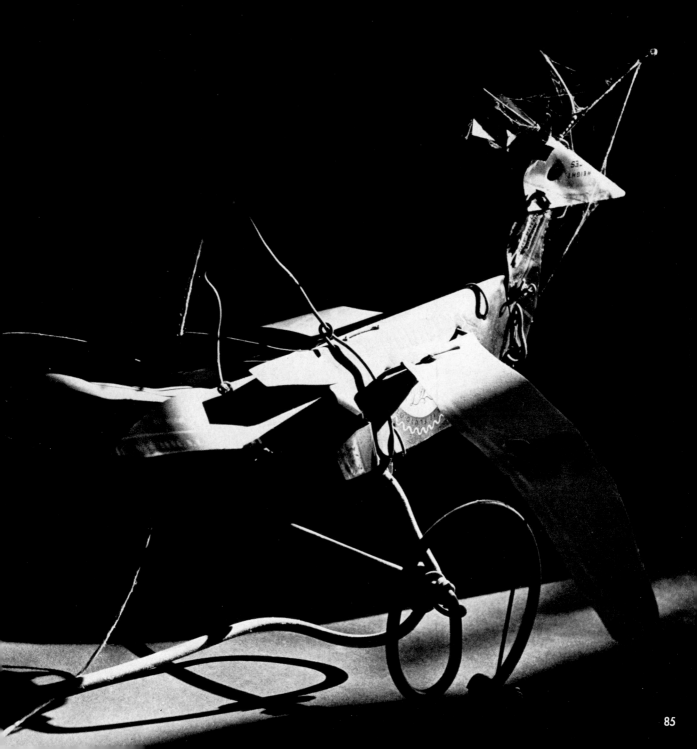

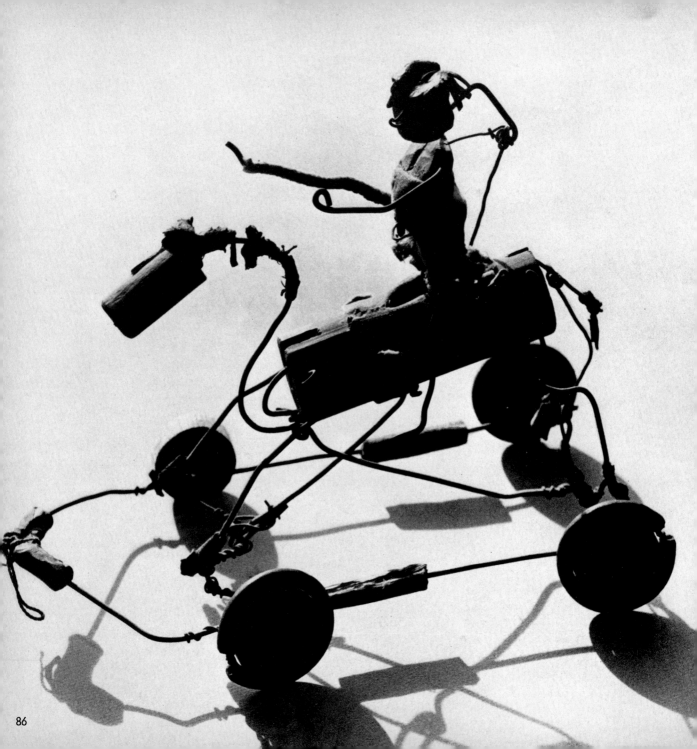

98

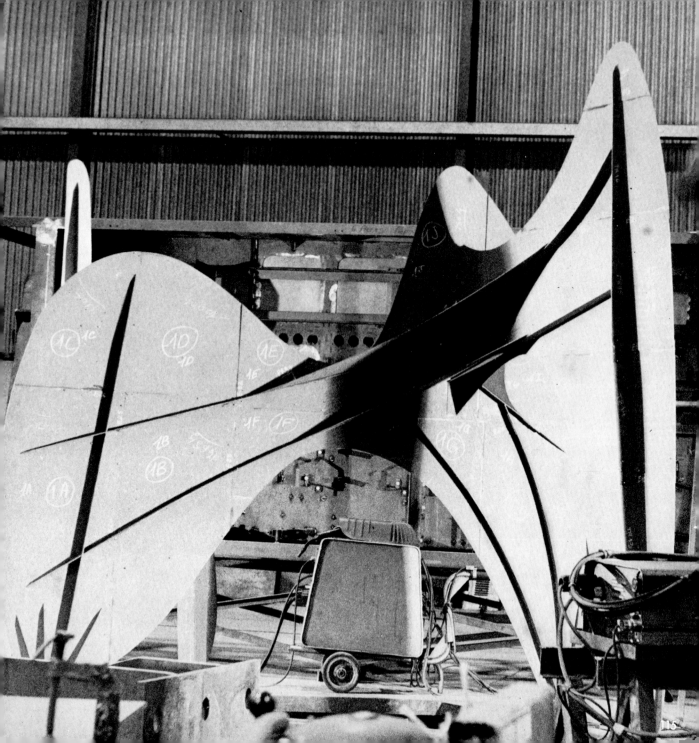